Corporate Collections in Montgomery

Corporate Collections in Montgomery

Montgomery Museum of Fine Arts
Montgomery, Alabama

May 15 through June 20, 1976

TABLE OF CONTENTS

INTRODUCTION

Many corporations throughout Europe and the United States have formed serious collections of art. In America, Westinghouse, Neiman-Marcus, and the Chase Manhattan Bank were a few of the forerunners to this phenomenon which has gained important new momentum. There are significant reasons for the development of corporate collections. A recent survey by Boston University pointed out that executives of thirty-five "art oriented" companies stressed that improving the corporate environment was a prime motivating factor for forming company collections. It is widely felt that employees working in an environment with art collections yield greater productivity and create strong corporate identities through the collection.

Funded by a grant from the Alabama State Council on the Arts and Humanities, the Montgomery Museum of Fine Arts undertook the first survey of corporate collections in the state of Alabama. This research revealed that the greatest concentration of corporate collections exists in the capitol city, with isolated collections in other locations. The strength of these collections is apparent. We have selected five firms from Montgomery to participate in the show, which reflects a broad range of diversity and emphasis. Limiting each company to ten works was extremely difficult, but the exhibition was selected to give one an introduction to these collections, as opposed to presenting definitive statements concerning each.

I would like to offer my sincerest thanks to the following individuals and corporations for their valuable assistance and cooperation in developing the exhibition: Mr. Winton Blount and Mr. Holman Head, Blount, Inc.; Mr. John Neill, Jr., Union Bank and Trust Company; Mr. Frank Plummer and Ms. Jen Mooney, First Alabama Bank of Montgomery; Mr. Hugh Smith, Hugh Smith Enterprises; and Mr. Adolph Weil, Jr. and Mr. Robert Weil, Weil Brothers-Cotton, Inc. Each has had to make special arrangements on several occasions for which the Museum is very grateful.

Henry Flood Robert, Jr.
Director

Blount, Inc.

Charles Burchfield   *Scrapped Locomotives*

Stuart Davis

Summer Twilight

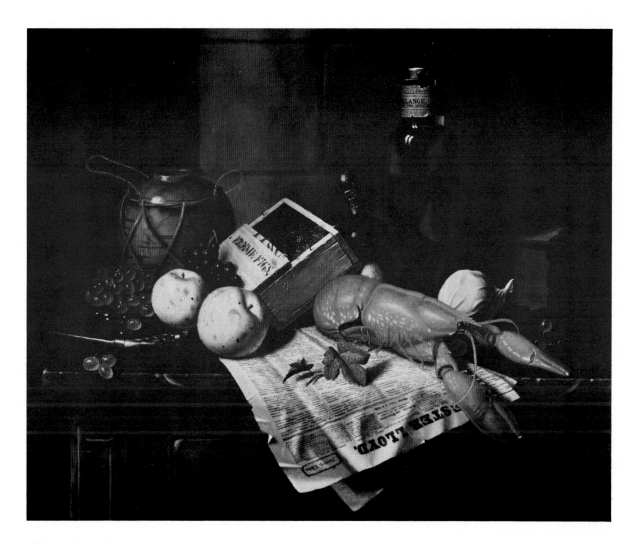

William Michael Harnett

Still Life with Lobster and Pester Lloyd

Edward Hopper

Light at Two Lights

Walt Kuhn

Clown with Long Nose

Maurice Prendergast

Dock Scene

CATALOG*

1. Charles Burchfield (1893-1967)
    Scrapped Locomotives
    19³/₄ x 29
    Watercolor

2. Stuart Davis (1894-1964)
    Summer Twilight
    35¹/₂ x 23¹/₂
    Oil on canvas

3. William Michael Harnett (1848-1892)
    Still Life with Lobster and Pester Lloyd
    13 x 16
    Oil on canvas

4. Childe Hassam, N.A. (1859-1935)
    Gloucester Harbor
    19¹/₂ x 23¹/₂
    Oil on canvas

5. Edward Hopper (1882-1967)
    Light at Two Lights
    13³/₄ x 19¹/₂
    Watercolor

6. Walt Kuhn (1877-1949)
    Clown with Long Nose
    39 x 29¹/₂
    Oil on canvas

7. Jack Levine (b. 1915)
    Election Night II
    19³/₄ x 23³/₄
    Oil on canvas

8. Reginald Marsh, N.A. (1898-1954)
    Sand Hogs
    49 x 29¹/₄
    Oil on canvas

9. Maurice Prendergast (1859-1924)
    Dock Scene
    15 x 22
    Watercolor

10. Ben Shahn (1898-1969)
    Italian Landscape II: Europa
    22 x 30
    Tempera

* Dimensions are given in inches.
  Height precedes width.

BIOGRAPHIES

1. ## Charles Burchfield (1893-1967)

Charles Burchfield was born in Ashtabula Harbor, Ohio on April 9, 1893. He began his art studies at the Cleveland Museum School of Art and continued on scholarship at the National Academy of Design, where he attended only one class. In 1921 he settled in Buffalo and worked as a wallpaper designer. Here he observed the post-war economic depression of an industrial city, an environment which found expression in his art in symbols and scenes of abandoned and desolate industry. A more romantic and poetic character pervaded later paintings as Burchfield turned to nature's changing moods and seasons for inspiration. His paintings have been exhibited in one-man shows at The Art Institute of Chicago; The Grosvenor Gallery, London; The Museum of Modern Art, New York; the Carnegie Institute, Pittsburgh; the Whitney Museum of American Art, New York; and others. Since his death in 1967, memorial exhibitions have been hung at the American Academy of Arts and Letters, New York and the Munson-Williams-Proctor Institute, New York. Burchfield taught at the University of Minnesota, the Art Institute of Buffalo, Ohio University, and Buffalo Fine Arts Academy. He was a member of the National Institute of Arts and Letters, and received a Gold Medal for Painting from the National Institute and the American Academy of Arts and Letters.

2. ## Stuart Davis (1894-1964)

Stuart Davis was born in Philadelphia, Pennsylvania on December 7, 1894 and, at the age of seven, moved to East Orange, New Jersey. Davis's father, art editor of *The (Philadelphia) Press,* was the supervisor of the artist-illustrators Shinn, Luks, Henri, and Sloan. It was his father who first introduced Davis to Henri, with whom he studied from 1910 to 1913. By 1920 Davis was moving away from the realistic subjects of *The Eight* toward a more abstract, cubistic, and simplified interpretation of forms painted in bright colors. He subsequently exhibited in the Exhibition of Independent Artists, New York; the Armory Show of 1913; and the Society of Independent Artists Annual. In the early part of his career, he contributed to *Harper's Weekly* and *The Masses.* In the 1930s he executed several mural commissions in New York, was part of the WPA Federal Art Project, New York, and was an editor for *Art Front.* He was a member of the faculty of The Art Students League of New York; the New School for Social Research, New York; Yale University, New Haven; and Famous Artists School, Connecticut. By 1917 one-man shows of his work were hung in New York to be followed by three exhibitions at the Whitney Studio Club and shows at The Museum of Modern Art, New York; Venice Biennale; Walker Art Center, Minneapolis; and others, with a memorial exhibition tour organized by the National Collection of Fine Arts, Smithsonian Institution in 1965. He was the recipient of two Guggenheim Foundation Fellowships, designed a Fine Arts Commemorative Stamp for the United States Post Office Department, and was awarded several medals including the Brandeis University Creative Arts Award Medal and the Fine Arts Gold Medal of the American Institute of Architecture. He belonged to the Artists' Union, the American Artists' Congress, and the National Institute of Arts and Letters. Stuart Davis died in New York on June 24, 1964.

3. ## William Michael Harnett (1848-1892)

William Michael Harnett was born in Clonakilty, Ireland in 1848. As a child he moved to Philadelphia with his family and later worked there as an engraver of table silver. He studied briefly at the Pennsylvania Academy of The Fine Arts, the National Academy of Design, and Cooper Union School of Art, New York. In 1874 he abandoned the silver trade for painting and the following year exhibited for the first time at the National Academy of Design. The years 1880 to 1886 were spent traveling in England, France, and Germany with a four-year stay in Munich. Harnett's reputation among contemporary art critics and established collectors was minimal. After his death in 1892, works by fellow still life artists were circulated with forged signatures of William Michael Harnett. Recent research by Dr.

Alfred Frankenstein has demonstrated that John F. Peto, a friend and pupil of Harnett, was responsible for signing the master's name to his own work. In 1939 there was a one-man show at the Downtown Gallery, New York. Harnett's work is in private and public collections such as the California Palace of the Legion of Honor, San Francisco; Museum of Fine Arts, Boston; and The Metropolitan Museum of Art, New York.

4. Childe Hassam, N.A. (1859-1935)

Childe Hassam was born in Dorchester, Massachusetts on October 17, 1859. He first worked for the publishers Little, Brown and Company and then became an apprentice for a Boston wood engraver. In the 1870s he studied painting with Ignaz Gaugengigl, attended classes at the Boston Art Club and Lowell Institute, and contributed illustrations to *Harper's, Century, Scribner's,* and others. The years 1886 to 1889 were spent in Paris as a student at the Académie Julian under Gustave Boulanger and Jules Lefebvre. It was at this time that he became interested in the Impressionists' theories and techniques of painting and decided to discard the academic principles taught at the Académie in favor of the former. Upon his return to the United States, Hassam, J. Alden Weir, and John Twachtman co-founded *The Ten,* a group of American Impressionists. He was elected an academician of the National Academy of Design in 1906, and was a member of the American Academy of Arts and Letters and the Association of Société Nationale des Beaux-Arts. He received more than thirty honors, awards, and medals during his lifetime, including prizes from the Exposition Universelle de 1889, Paris; the Pan-American Exposition, Buffalo; Second and First Altman Prize; and the Saltus Medal. Paintings by the artist were also included in the Armory Show of 1913 and in the Society of Independent Artists Annual in 1917. His work has been the subject of many retrospectives and one-man shows, the first being held in Boston in 1883. Subsequent exhibitions were hung at the Durand-Ruel Galleries, New York; the Albright Art Gallery, Buffalo; the Corcoran Gallery of Art, Washington, D.C.; and the University of Arizona Art Gallery, Tucson. The artist died at his summer home in Easthampton, Long Island on August 27, 1935.

5. Edward Hopper (1882-1967)

Edward Hopper was born in Nyack, New York on July 22, 1882. He studied illustration at a commercial art school before attending the New York School of Art, where his instructors were Robert Henri, George Luks, and Kenneth Hayes Miller. He exhibited his American scene paintings in numerous New York group shows during the first decades of the twentieth century such as the Original Independent Show of 1908, the Exhibition of Independent Artists, and the Armory Show of 1913, but did not achieve national recognition until about 1920. He was offered membership in the National Academy of Design in 1932, but he declined because of its rejection of his work in the past. His first one-man exhibition was held at the Whitney Studio Club in 1920. It was followed by other one-man shows and major retrospectives at The Museum of Modern Art, New York; Carnegie Institute, Pittsburgh; Whitney Museum of American Art, New York; and the Philadelphia Museum of Art. Among the many awards and prizes he received during his lifetime were the Corcoran Gold Medal and First Clark Prize, Corcoran Biennial; Logan Medal, The Art Institute of Chicago; Gold Medal for Painting, the National Institute of Arts and Letters, and the American Academy of Arts and Letters. He was a member of the National Institute of Arts and Letters and the American Academy of Arts and Letters. He died in New York City on May 15, 1967. After the death of his wife, his entire artistic estate was bequeathed to the Whitney Museum of American Art.

6. Walt Kuhn (1877-1949)

Walt Kuhn was born in Brooklyn, New York on October 27, 1877. He attended evening classes at the Polytechnic Institute of Brooklyn. His education continued at the Académie Colarossi in Paris and at the Royal Academy in Munich. At various times, Kuhn worked as a cartoonist for *Life, Puck, New York Sunday Sun,* and *New York World;* director of musical reviews; advisor to art collectors John Quinn and Lillie P. Bliss; consulting architect for the Union Pacific Railroad; and served on the faculty of The Art Students League of New York and the New York School of Art. As executive secretary of the Association of American Painters and Sculptors, he was an influential figure in the organization of the Armory Show. Arthur B. Davies, Walter Pach, and Kuhn met in Europe to represent the Armory Show and choose the foreign section of the exhibition. Kuhn's first one-man show in New York preceded the Armory Show and was followed by other one-man and group shows throughout the United States. Although he painted landscapes, portraits, and still lifes, he is best known for his paintings of clowns and the world of circus performers. A retrospective was held at the Durand-Ruel Galleries, New York in 1949. During the 1960s exhibitions were hung at the Cincinnati Art Museum; Maynard Walker Gallery, New York; University of Arizona Art Gallery, Tucson; and the Kennedy Galleries, New York. Walt Kuhn died in White Plains, New York on July 13, 1949.

7. Jack Levine (b. 1915)

Jack Levine was born in Boston, Massachusetts on January 3, 1915. At the age of nine he took his first art lessons with Harold Zimmerman at the Boston Museum of Fine Arts and later worked under the tutelage of Denman Ross at Harvard University. From 1935 to 1940 he was a member of the WPA Federal Art Project, Easel Division. In 1939 he had his first one-man show at the Downtown Gallery, New York resulting in participation in group exhibitions such as *New Horizons in American Art,* The Museum of Modern Art, New York and *Portrait of America,* The Metropolitan Museum of Art, New York. In 1945 and 1947 he was the recipient of Guggenheim Foundation Fellowships; in 1946, a grant from the American Academy of Arts and Sciences; and in 1950-1951, a Fulbright Grant. As one of the foremost American painters of political satire and social commentary, he has been represented in national and international group exhibitions. He has taught at the Pennsylvania Academy of The

Fine Arts and at the Skowhegan School of Painting and Sculpture, Maine where he now serves as a member of the Board of Governors. Retrospectives have been hung at the Institute of Contemporary Art, Boston; the I Bienal Interamericana, Mexico City; and the De Cordova and Dana Museum, Massachusetts. He is a member of the National Institute of Arts and Letters and the American Academy of Arts and Letters. Jack Levine lives in New York.

8. Reginald Marsh, N.A. (1898-1954)

Reginald Marsh was born on March 14, 1898 of American parents who, at the time of his birth, were studying art in Paris. He returned to the United States with his family in 1900 and graduated from Yale University in 1920. His studies were continued at The Art Students League of New York under John Sloan, Kenneth Hayes Miller, George Luks, and George B. Bridgman which led to his association with the 14th Street School of Painters. During the 1920s he worked as an illustrator for several New York newspapers and periodicals, including the *New York Evening Post, New York Herald, Vanity Fair, Harper's Bazaar,* the New York *Daily News,* and *The New Yorker.* The years 1933 and 1934 were spent working for the Public Works of Art Project Mural Division in New York; in 1936 he received additional WPA mural commissions from the U.S. Treasury Department, Section of Fine Arts and Treasury Relief Art Project for the Washington, D.C. Post Office. The artist was an instructor at The Art Students League and at the Moore Institute of Art, Science and Industry in Philadelphia in the 1940s and 1950s, and served as a wartime artist-correspondent for a short period for *Life.* He became a member of the Whitney Studio Club in New York in 1923; was a vice-president of The Art Students League in 1933-1934; and was elected an associate member of the National Academy of Design in 1937 and an academician in 1943. His membership in the National Institute of Arts and Letters began in 1946. The first of many one-man shows was hung at the Whitney Studio Club in 1924. Among the prizes and medals awarded to Marsh were the

Kohnstamm Prize and the Blair Prize from The Art Institute of Chicago, the Clarke Prize from the National Academy of Design, the Corcoran Gold Medal and the First Clark Prize at the Corcoran Biennial and the Gold Medal for Graphic Arts, the National Institute of Arts and Letters. After his death in 1954 the Whitney Museum of American Art organized a memorial exhibition and tour; a retrospective was shown in 1969 at the University of Arizona Art Gallery in Tucson.

9. Maurice Prendergast (1859-1924)

Maurice Prendergast was born in St. John's, Newfoundland on October 10, 1859 and two years later moved to Boston with his family. After an apprenticeship to a painter of show cards, he worked his way to Europe on a cattle boat. This stay in 1886 was brief, but was followed by an extended period in 1891 at which time he studied in Paris at the Académie Colarossi and Académie Julian. Returning to the United States in 1894, he managed a frame shop with his brother Charles. He was a member of *The Eight,* a group of realist painters who had a single exhibition at the Macbeth Gallery, New York in 1908, and later showed jointly with other artists from the exhibition. Unlike other members of *The Eight,* Prendergast used the Impressionist palette and technique. He was vice-president of the Society of Independent Artists, an organization formed in 1917 to provide an additional opportunity for artists to exhibit their work. In 1917 he moved to New York and remained there until his death in 1924. The artist's work is included in major museum collections in the United States. He received numerous prizes and awards during his life from institutions such as the Corcoran Gallery of Art, Washington, D.C. He had one-man exhibitions in Boston, Ohio, and New York. A memorial exhibition was organized by the Cleveland Museum of Art in 1926 and retrospectives have been hung at the Whitney Museum of American Art, New York; the Museum of Fine Arts, Boston; and M. Knoedler and Company, New York.

10. Ben Shahn (1898-1969)

Ben Shahn was born in Kovno, Lithuania on September 12, 1898. In 1906 he emigrated to Brooklyn with his family. At the age of thirteen he became a lithographer's apprentice and worked intermittently in this field while he pursued his artistic studies at the Educational Alliance in New York, New York University, the City College of New York, the National Academy of Design, The Art Students League of New York, and the Académie de la Grande Chaumière, Paris. In the 1930s he assisted the Mexican muralist Diego Rivera on works for the RCA Building, Rockefeller Center; was on the editorial staff of *Art Front;* and worked as a photographer for the Farm Security Administration. The association with Rivera may have contributed to the development of his individualistic art expression of a social-realism that commented on contemporary political and social issues. During World War II he served as a senior liaison officer, Graphics Division, Office of War Information and then became Director of the Graphic Arts Division, C.I.O. He served on the faculty of the School of the Museum of Fine Arts, Boston; the University of Colorado, Boulder; The Brooklyn Museum Art School; the Black Mountain College, North Carolina; and was appointed the Norton Professor of Poetry at Harvard University. Volumes which he illustrated include *The Alphabet of Creation, The Shape of Content,* and *Ecclesiastes, or the Preacher.* The first of many one-man shows was held at the Downtown Gallery, New York in 1930 and was followed by shows at museums and galleries in Boston, London, New York, Pennsylvania, and Washington, D.C. He was the recipient of a number of awards and prizes such as the Purchase Prize from the II São Paolo Bienal; the American Institute of Graphic Arts Medal; and the Gold Medal for Graphic Art, the National Institute of Arts and Letters, and the American Academy of Arts and Letters. He was a member of the latter two organizations. After his death in 1969, retrospectives were organized by the New Jersey State Museum and the Ishibashi Memorial Hall, Kurume, Japan.

First Alabama Bank of Montgomery

Hélèna Adamoff

Marche aux Fleurs

Vu Cao Dam   *Maternité*

Jean Dufy   *Venise*

Doris Kennedy

Untitled

Constantin Kluge   *L'Ile de Lutece*

Gérard Passet

Chemin du Village

CATALOG*

1. Héléna Adamoff (b. 1906)
   Marche aux Fleurs
   $14^1/_2$ x 21
   Oil on canvas

2. Yolande Ardissone (b. 1927)
   Kerbernique
   28 x $35^1/_2$
   Oil on canvas

3. John Bentham-Dinsdale (b. 1927)
   The Rainbow
   $29^1/_4$ x 39
   Oil on canvas

4. Bernard Buffet (b. 1928)
   Phare et Barque Rouge
   $25^1/_4$ x $19^1/_2$
   Watercolor

5. Vu Cao Dam (b. 1908)
   Maternité
   10 x 8
   Oil on canvas

6. Jean Dufy (1888-1964)
   Venise
   $13^1/_4$ x 27
   Watercolor

7. Doris Kennedy (b. 1916)
   Untitled
   17 x $11^1/_2$
   Watercolor

8. Constantin Kluge (b. 1912)
   L'Ile de Lutece
   $23^1/_2$ x $35^1/_2$
   Oil on canvas

9. Ljubomir Milinkov (20th cen.)
   Untitled
   $9^1/_2$ x $7^1/_2$
   Oil on canvas

10. Gérard Passet (b. 1936)
    Chemin du Village
    29 x $35^1/_2$
    Oil on canvas

* Dimensions are given in inches.
  Height precedes width.

BIOGRAPHIES

1. Hélèna Adamoff (b. 1906)

Hélèna Adamoff was born in Moscow on May 21, 1906. She moved to France at the age of fifteen and has resided there since. Her first painting was executed in 1956 at the age of fifty while she was convalescing from an accident. A modern primitive painter, she portrays an unreal world of her own vision in a naive unsophisticated manner. The artist has had no formal training. Her Russian childhood is often reflected in her choice of subjects, in particular, the landscapes and costumes. She was included in a group show in 1956, the year she began painting, and has since participated in group shows in France, Austria, England, Scotland, and Wales, as well as in Salons such as the Salon Comparaisons, the Salon des Indépendants, the Salon des Artistes Français, the Salon d'Automne, and the Salon des Femmes Peintres.

2. Yolande Ardissone (b. 1927)

Yolande Ardissone was born of an Italian father and Russian mother in Normandy in 1927. At the age of seventeen she moved to Paris to study at the Ecole des Arts Appliqués and the Académie de la Grande Chaumière, and transferred two years later to the Ecole des Beaux-Arts, atelier of Unterseller, and the City of Paris art school. The first exhibit of her work was in the Salon des Artistes Francais in 1950. She was awarded an honorable mention and subsequently was elected a member of the Salon. Major Salons in which she has shown are the Salon d'Automne, the Salon de la Société Nationale des Beaux-Arts, the Salon des Indépendants, and the Grands et Jeunes d'Aujourd'hui. She has participated in group exhibitions in France such as Les Peintres Témoins de leur Temps, and Société des Amateurs d'Art as well as in shows in England, Italy, Sweden, Venezuela, Switzerland, Germany, Canada, and Belgium. In 1957 she was awarded the Médaille d'Argent de la Ville de Paris and in 1967 the Prix de la Ville de Fontainebleau. Her work is included in both private and public collections in the United States and France. Yolande Ardissone has traveled extensively but often returns to the picturesque landscape of Brittany, her summer residence, for her painting subject.

3. John Bentham-Dinsdale (b. 1927)

John Bentham-Dinsdale was born in Ilkley, Yorkshire, England on December 9, 1927. He was educated at Bridlington College and Ashville College and received a Diploma in Architecture from the Leeds School of Art. Although he has always been interested in painting, it was not until 1965 that marine painting became his primary interest. This is complemented by his study of naval and marine history. His paintings are in collections in Britain, the United States, Australia, Sweden, Japan, and South Africa.

4. Bernard Buffet (b. 1928)

Bernard Buffet was born in Paris on July 10, 1928. Buffet received his brief formal art instruction during evening drawing classes at the City of Paris in 1943 and at the Ecole des Beaux-Arts. The year 1944 marked his public debut at the Salon des Moins de Trente Ans and from that time forth he participated in numerous Salons, including the Salon des Indépendants, Salon d'Automne, Salon de l'Ecole de Paris, and the Biennale Internationale de la Jeune Peinture. In 1947 his first one-man show was held at the Galerie des Impressions d'Art, and in 1948 he was awarded the Prix de la Critique with Bernard Lorjou at the Galerie St. Placide. During the 1940s the movement known as Misérablisme affected his style. The following years brought numerous one-man exhibitions throughout the United States and Europe. In 1958 at the age of thirty, a retrospective exhibition was shown at the Galerie Charpentier. Buffet, a member of the major French Salons, executed décors for several ballets including Françoise Sagan's *Le Rendez-vous manqué* and has illustrated several books such as Jean Cocteau's *La Voix Humaine* and *La Passion* and Cyrano de Bergerac's *Le Voyage dans la Lune.* His paintings are in the collections of The Tate Gallery, London; the São Paolo Museum, Brazil; the Musée National d'Art Moderne, Paris; the Museum of Modern Art,

New York; The Art Institute of Chicago; and others. The unique style which characterizes the artist's work highlights linear and geometric compositional elements.

5. Vu Cao Dam (b. 1908)

Vu Cao Dam was born in Hanoi, Indo-China in 1908. He began his art studies at the Ecole des Beaux-Arts in Hanoi under Victor Boloubew. He left his native country for Paris in 1931 intending to continue in sculpture, but shortly thereafter decided to devote himself to painting. His compositions combine Asiatic subjects, primarily figurative, with European painterly techniques. Vu Cao Dam has exhibited at the Salon des Indépendants, the Salon des Tuileries, and the Salon d'Automne. He is represented in public and private collections in France and has had exhibitions in France, the Scandinavian countries, and the United States. One of his paintings was selected by UNICEF for a 1966 Christmas card. He remained in Paris from 1931 to 1949 and presently resides in the south of France.

6. Jean Dufy (1888-1964)

Jean Dufy was born at Seine Inférieure near Le Havre on March 12, 1888. Like his older brother Raoul, Jean studied at the Ecole des Beaux-Arts du Havre. He later traveled to Paris where he studied with his brother's former teacher, Othon Friesz, and had the opportunity to meet, through Raoul, the artists Braque, Rouault, Vlaminck, and Marquet. By 1920 he had exhibited his work and was gaining additional experience in other artistic mediums by designing textiles for the Lyons silk manufacturers and decorating Limoges porcelain. He left Paris after a misunderstanding with his brother about a mural executed for the Palace of Electricity at the 1937 Paris World's Fair. He and his wife moved to the region of Loire where he lived until his death in 1964, except for intervals of travel throughout Europe. The artist was a member of the Salon d'Automne and periodically exhibited there.

7. Doris Kennedy (b. 1916)

Doris Kennedy was born in Bernice, Louisiana on January 26, 1916. She received her Bachelor of Arts degree from Louisiana Polytechnic Institute and was an art instructor in the Birmingham, Alabama public schools for five years. She has exhibited extensively throughout the South and at the Art Collectors Gallery in Mexico City. Her watercolors have been awarded prizes from the Birmingham Museum of Art; Butler Institute of American Art, Ohio; and the Southeastern Annual. The artist is a member of the Philadelphia Watercolor Club, Audubon Artists, Alabama Watercolor Society, and the Birmingham Art Association. Several public collections in which her work is represented are the Springfield Museum of Art, Massachusetts; Butler Institute of American Art, Ohio; Birmingham Museum of Art, Alabama; and the University of Tennessee, Nashville. The artist presently resides in Birmingham, Alabama.

8. Constantin Kluge (b. 1912)

Constantin Kluge was born in Riga in 1912, spent his childhood in Russia, and at the age of eight emigrated with his parents to Shanghai, China. He graduated from the French Municipal College in Shanghai in 1931, and completed his studies in architecture at the Ecole des Beaux-Arts in Paris with the title of French Government Architect in 1937. He prolonged his stay in the French capital for six months using the time to paint scenes of the city in oil, a subject that would reappear in his art. He returned to China to practice architecture but shortly thereafter decided to devote himself exclusively to painting. He left China for Paris at the start of the Sino-Japanese War and has remained there since that time. His first award from the Paris Salon was received in 1951; additional honors include the Médaille d'Argent and the special Raymond Perreau prize given by the Taylor Foundation, and the Gold Medal from the 1962 Salon. He has had several one-man shows in the United States and Paris at the Wally Findlay Galleries and has exhibited at the Salon of the Société des Artistes Francais.

9. Ljubomir Milinkov (20th cen.)

Ljubomir Milinkov was born in Valjevo, near Belgrade, Yugoslavia. He left the country of his birth in 1960 to study art in France and in 1968 he emigrated to the United States. Primarily a painter of the peasants and countryside of Yugoslavia, he was strongly influenced by the Primitive school of paintings centered in Hlebinje, Generalic. He has exhibited in Belgrade, Paris, Rome, Brussels, and the United States.

10. Gérard Passet (b. 1936)

Gérard Passet was born at Villeneuve-le-roi, near Paris, in 1936. His formal art studies were under Marcel Roche, Goerg, and then with Yves Brayer at the Grande Chaumière. His first exhibition was in the Salon d'Automne in Paris in 1956 and was followed by participation in the principal Salons and exhibitions in France, Italy, Canada, Japan, the United States, and England. Passet's paintings of villages and country roads of Northern France and the Ile de France are in numerous private collections in France and abroad and in the collections of the French State. The artist presently resides in France.

Hugh Smith Enterprises

Albert Bierstadt, N.A.

Buffalo Hunt on the Prairie

Richard Creifields   *Landscape*

George Luks

Central Park Lake

Edward Moran

A Shipwreck

Robert Reid, N.A.   *A Woman*

Attrib. to Borlase Smart   *Marine Painting*

CATALOG*

1. Albert Bierstadt, N.A. (1830-1902)
   Buffalo Hunt on the Prairie
   25³/₄ x 36
   Oil on canvas

2. Richard Creifields (1853-1939)
   Landscape
   17¹/₂ x 21¹/₂
   Oil on canvas

3. Richard Creifields (1853-1939)
   Landscape
   17 x 21
   Oil on canvas

4. Ernest Lawson, N.A. (1873-1939)
   Colorado Scene on the Road to Cripple Creek
   15¹/₂ x 19¹/₂
   Oil on canvas

5. George Luks (1866-1933)
   Central Park Lake
   31 x 34
   Oil on canvas

6. George Luks (1866-1933)
   Storm in the Bronx
   24¹/₂ x 29³/₄
   Oil on canvas

7. Edward Moran (1829-1901)
   A Shipwreck
   29¹/₂ x 44¹/₂
   Oil on canvas

8. Robert Reid, N.A. (1862-1929)
   A Woman
   23¹/₂ x 17¹/₂
   Pastel

9. Attrib. to Borlase Smart (1881-?)
   Marine Painting
   26 x 39¹/₄
   Oil on canvas

10. Attrib. to Borlase Smart (1881-?)
    Marine Painting
    23¹/₂ x 39¹/₂
    Oil on canvas

* Dimensions are given in inches.
Height precedes width.

BIOGRAPHIES

1. ### Albert Bierstadt, N.A. (1830-1902)

    Albert Bierstadt was born in Solingen, Germany on January 7, 1830 and emigrated with his family to Massachusetts in 1832. He later returned to Dusseldorf to study under Emanuel Leutze, Carl Friedrich Lessing, and Andreas Achenbach. Before returning to the United States, he toured Germany, Italy, and Switzerland. Shortly after his return to the states, he became a member of a Pacific Coast States Railway Survey expedition in the West. On this and other trips through the North Platte and Wyoming Territory, he had the opportunity to study the country's topography and scenery and make sketches, stereographs, and photographs. In the 1860s he painted his first panoramic western landscape, the style of painting for which he became known. He paid an exemption fee to free himself from Civil War military service, but visited Union Army camps to record the scenes of war in sketches. He later worked with the American photographer Eadweard Muybridge. During the years 1858 through 1893, he exhibited at the National Academy of Design Annual Exhibitions, the Philadelphia Centennial Exposition, the London Royal Academy of Arts Annual, the World's Columbian Exposition in Chicago, and others. Eighteen hundred eighty-nine, the year in which the New York artists' committee refused to send *Last of the Buffalo* to the Paris Exposition, marked the decline of his popularity and the beginning of his financial problems. He died in New York on February 18, 1902.

2. ### Richard Creifields (1853-1939)

    Richard Creifields was born in New York in 1853. His art education was begun at the National Academy of Design and was continued in 1872 in Munich where he was a student of Barth and Alexander von Wagner. Paintings by Creifields are included in the collection of The Brooklyn Museum.

3. ### Richard Creifields

    See No. 2.

4. ### Ernest Lawson, N.A. (1873-1939)

    Ernest Lawson was born in Halifax, Nova Scotia on March 22, 1873. He worked as a draftsman in Mexico City in 1889 while studying at the Santa Clara Art Academy. He then moved to New York to study at The Art Students League of New York. His art instruction was continued at the summer art school directed by John Twachtman and J. Alden Weir in Cos Cob, Connecticut and completed at the Académie Julian, Paris in 1893 and 1894. In 1893 he exhibited in the Paris Salon. He was elected an associate of the National Academy of Design in 1908, and nine years later became an academician. Lawson participated in the exhibition of *The Eight* at the Macbeth Gallery in New York, which included Robert Henri and five of his students, and two additional artists, Prendergast and Lawson. The latter two artists utilized an impressionistic style which provided a poetic and picturesque overlay to the realistic and commonplace cityscapes painted by the other members of the show. Lawson taught at the University of Georgia, Columbus; Kansas City Art Institute and School of Design; and the Broadmoor Academy, Colorado. As part of the Federal Works Agency, Section of Fine Arts, he painted a mural for the United States Post Office in Short Hills, New Jersey. Among the awards and honors he received during his lifetime were the Silver Medal from the St. Louis International Exposition, Missouri; the Sesnan Gold Medal from the Pennsylvania Academy of The Fine Arts; the First Hallgarten Prize, National Academy of Design; and the Corcoran Silver Medal and Second Clark Prize, Corcoran Biennial. One-man exhibitions have been hung at numerous galleries and museums such as the Pennsylvania Academy, Nova Scotia Museum of Fine Arts, and the National Gallery of Canada, Ottawa. He died in Coral Gables, Florida on December 18, 1939.

5. ### George Luks (1866-1933)

    George Luks was born in Williamsport, Pennsylvania on August 13, 1866. He studied at the Pennsylvania Academy of The Fine Arts and at the Dusseldorf Art Academy. After a ten-year stay in Europe which included travels to Munich, Paris, and London, he returned to the United States to assume employment as artist-reporter for *The (Philadelphia) Press.* In 1896 the *Philadelphia Evening Bulletin* sent William Glackens and Luks to Cuba to cover the Spanish-American War. In Philadelphia he shared living quarters with Everett Shinn, knew John Sloan, and attended the weekly sessions at Robert Henri's studio. These artists, with the exception of Shinn, exhibited together for the first time at the National Arts Club in New York in 1904. Their realistic works, which challenged traditional academic interpretations, were consistently rejected by the National Academy of Design and the Society of American Artists. In 1908 a counter exhibition to the National Academy Annual was held at the Macbeth Gallery in which the Philadelphia artists were joined by Maurice Prendergast, Ernest Lawson, and Arthur B. Davies. This group came to be known as *The Eight.* Luks taught at The Art Students League of New York from 1920 to 1924 and later founded his own school in New York. His work was hung in one-man shows in the East and has been included in major exhibitions of American art. After his death in 1933 a memorial exhibition was hung at the Newark Museum. Among the awards he received were the Temple Gold Medal, Pennsylvania Academy of The Fine Arts; the Logan Medal, The Art Institute of Chicago; and the First William A. Clark Prize and Gold Medal, Corcoran Gallery of Art. He was a member of the American Society of Painters, Sculptors, and Gravers; the National Association of Portrait Painters; and the New York Society of Artists. George Luks died in New York on October 29, 1933.

6. George Luks

   See No. 5.

7. Edward Moran (1829-1901)

   Edward Moran was born in Bolton, England on August 19, 1829. He left England for the United States as a young boy, and settled in Philadelphia where he received his first art instruction. He later returned to England to work at the school of the Royal Academy. Before returning to the United States in 1877, he traveled to Paris. He then established himself in New York. Edward was the older brother of Thomas Moran, an American landscape artist, to whom he taught the basic principles of painting. He was a member of the Pennsylvania Academy of The Fine Arts and exhibited in Philadelphia in 1853. He died in New York on June 9, 1901.

8. Robert Reid, N.A. (1862-1929)

   Robert Reid was born in Stockbridge, Massachusetts on July 29, 1862. His art education included four years of study at the Boston Museum School, a brief period at The Art Students League of New York, and four years at the Académie Julian under Gustave Boulanger and Jules Lefebvre. He returned to the United States in 1889 and in 1898 was instrumental in the founding of *The Ten,* a group of American artists who joined together to protest current academic practices. The artist, who is known for his murals and paintings of idealized women, executed commissons for the Liberal Arts Building of the World's Columbian Exposition, Chicago; the Library of Congress; the Boston State House; and the Palace of Fine Arts, Panama-Pacific Exposition, San Francisco. He participated in shows such as the Exposition Universelle, Paris; the Pan-American Exposition, Buffalo; Macbeth Gallery, New York; and the National Academy of Design. Awards and prizes for these exhibitions and others included the First Hallgarten Prize, National Academy of Design; Gold and Silver Medals from the Exposition Universelle; and a Gold Medal from the Panama-Pacific Exposition. In 1906 he was elected a member of the National Academy of Design. Institutions at which he taught were Cooper Union School of Art, The Art Students League, and Broadmoor Art Academy, Colorado. Reid died on December 2, 1929 in Clifton Springs, New York.

9. Borlase Smart (b. 1881)

Borlase Smart was born in Kingsbridge, Devonshire, England on February 11, 1881. He was a student of the English marine painter Julius Olsson. Drawings by Smart are located at the Imperial War Museum of London and Plymouth.

10. Attributed to Borlase Smart

See No. 9.

Union Bank and Trust Company

J. Kelly Fitzpatrick

Bream Fishermen - Old Camp Dixie

Barbara Gallagher

Beethoven's Fifth

Dean Gillette

Morning Transparencies

Ida Kohlmeyer

Tabulated

Virginia R. Rogers   *Hats*

Clark Walker

Man in Yellow Hat

CATALOG*

1. J. Kelly Fitzpatrick (1888-1953)
   Bream Fishermen - Old Camp Dixie
   $8^1/_4$ x $11^3/_4$
   Watercolor

2. Mary Virginia Fuller (b. 1918)
   Which Came First?
   $13^3/_4$ x 17
   Oil on masonite

3. Barbara Gallagher (b. 1933)
   Beethoven's Fifth
   $47^1/_2$ x $49^1/_2$
   Acrylic on canvas

4. Dean Gillette (b. 1930)
   Morning Transparencies
   42 x 38
   Acrylic on canvas

5. Anne Goldthwaite (1870-1944)
   Mules
   $15^3/_4$ x $19^1/_2$
   Watercolor

6. Oswaldo Guayasamin (b. 1919)
   Landscape of Quito
   $47^1/_2$ x $47^1/_2$
   Oil on canvas

7. Ida Kohlmeyer (b. 1912)
   Tabulated
   46 x $49^3/_4$
   Oil on canvas

8. Virginia R. Rogers (20th cen.)
   Hats
   $25^1/_2$ x $31^1/_2$
   Oil on canvas

9. John Wagnon (b. 1933)
   Winona Creek
   19 x $23^1/_2$
   Oil on canvas

10. Clark Walker (b. 1940)
    Man in Yellow Hat
    $39^1/_2$ x $39^1/_2$
    Acrylic on canvas

* Dimensions are given in inches.
Height precedes width.

BIOGRAPHIES

1. ## J. Kelly Fitzpatrick (1888-1953)

    John Kelly Fitzpatrick was born in Wetumpka, Alabama on August 15, 1888. He began his studies at the University of Alabama and continued at The Art Institute of Chicago in 1912 and at the Académie Julian in Paris in 1926. Fitzpatrick, instrumental in founding the Alabama Art League in 1930 and president for eleven successive years, was also a founder of the Montgomery Museum of Fine Arts and director of the Museum's Art School from its beginning in 1930 to his death in 1958. In addition, he founded the Dixie Art Colony and the Bayou Art Colony and served as an instructor at both institutions. In 1933 he represented Alabama in the *American Scene* exhibition at the John Herron Art Institute in Indiana, and in 1935 represented his home state in the Grumbacher *Gallery of States* traveling exhibition. He was included in the *American Art Today* exhibition at the New York World's Fair of 1939 and in the Public Works of Art Project. A painting from the latter exhibition was admired by General Eisenhower and later hung in his presidential office. He exhibited extensively in Alabama and throughout the South and was the recipient of numerous awards and honors. Paintings by the artist are in the collections of the Alabama State Capitol, the Montgomery Museum of Fine Arts, International Business Machines Corporation, Grumbacher, the American Artist Palette Collection, and the Loveman Collection. He was a member of many Southern art organizations such as the Southern States Art League, the Arts Association of New Orleans, and the Alabama Art Commission. J. Kelly Fitzpatrick died in 1953.

2. ## Mary Virginia Fuller (b. 1918)

    Mary Virginia Fuller was born in San Antonio, Texas on February 15, 1918. She studied history at Trinity University. The artist, who has had no formal art instruction, has been painting for approximately twenty years. During the past ten years she has been working in a traditional oil technique using glazes on a prepared board. The artist's realistic still lifes have been exhibited in various local and regional shows and have received many purchase awards. Her art is represented in many Southern private collections.

3. ## Barbara Gallagher (b. 1933)

    Barbara Gallagher was born in Tuscaloosa, Alabama in August, 1933. Her Bachelor of Fine Arts degree was earned at the University of Alabama. She has exhibited frequently in Southern local and regional shows and her acrylic paintings and wood mosaics have been awared prizes from exhibitions such as the Montgomery Art Guild Annual Exhibition and the 1974 Alabama Art League Forty-Fifth Annual Juried Exhibition. The artist presently resides in Montgomery where she is active in community cultural events. She is a Board Member of the Montgomery Museum of Fine Arts Association, organized the major city art festival in 1975, and has designed costumes and sets for the Montgomery Civic Ballet. A studio-gallery is maintained in Montgomery where she teaches classes in painting. A one-woman show was hung at the Montgomery Museum in 1971. Works by Barbara Gallagher are in local and national private collections.

4. ## Dean Gillette (b. 1930)

    Dean Gillette was born in Parsons, Kansas on December 13, 1930. He studied at the Kansas City Art Institute in Missouri before attending the University of Kansas where he received his first Bachelor of Fine Arts degree. He graduated with a second Bachelor of Fine Arts degree and a Master of Fine Arts degree from Yale University in 1955 and 1957 respectively. He continued his education at the University of London and with Josef Albers, Conrad Marca-Relli, and Burgoine Diller. Gillette's first one-man show was held at the Bodley Gallery in New York in 1966 and has been followed by participation in group exhibitions and one-man shows in cities such as Philadelphia, Atlanta, New Orleans, Montgomery, and Washington, D.C. In 1974 he was selected by Alfred

Frankenstein to represent contemporary American painting at Expo '74 in Spokane, Washington. His work is in numerous private and public collections including the American Telephone and Telegraph Collection, New York; the Georgia Museum of Art; the High Museum of Art, Georgia; the William Rockhill Nelson Gallery of Art, Missouri; and the New Orleans Museum of Art. The artist has been a member of the Pennsylvania Academy of The Fine Arts since 1967.

5. Anne Goldthwaite (1870-1944)

Anne Goldthwaite was born in Montgomery, Alabama in 1870. At an early age she was sent to the National Academy of Design in New York to study under Walter Shirlaw and Charles W. Mielatz. In 1907 she enrolled in the Académie of Paris where she studied with Charles Guerin and Othon Friesz. In Paris she assisted in the founding of the Académie Moderne, a school established by young artists who broke with nineteenth century traditional painting, and met Gertrude Stein who introduced her to the work of Cézanne, Picasso, and Matisse. At the outbreak of World War I, she returned to the United States in time to participate in the Armory Show of 1913. Other exhibitions in which her work appeared were hung at the National Association of Women Painters and Sculptors. Knoedler Galleries, New York mounted a memorial exhibition in 1945, and Kennedy Galleries, New York organized a retrospective and tour in 1967. Oil paintings, watercolors, and etchings by Anne Goldthwaite can be found in the permanent collections of the Montgomery Museum of Fine Arts; Rhode Island School of Design, Museum of Art; The Metropolitan Museum of Art, New York; The Baltimore Museum of Art; Los Angeles County Museum of Art; the Whitney Museum of American Art, New York; and many other public and private collections. National recognition was achieved in 1915 with the receipt of the McMillan landscape prize awarded by the National Association of Women Painters and Sculptors and a bronze medal for etching at the Panama-Pacific Exposition in San Francisco. The artist, one of the best known painters of Southern subjects, died in New York City in 1944.

6. Oswaldo Guayasamin (b. 1919)

Oswaldo Guayasamin was born in Quito, Ecuador on July 6, 1919. He studied painting and sculpture at the National School of Fine Arts in Quito. In 1941 the first exhibition of his work was hung in Quito and was followed by participation in shows throughout the Americas. The United States Department of State invited Guayasamin to tour American museums in 1943 which coincided with exhibitions of South American artists at the City Art Museum, St. Louis; San Francisco Art Museum; and the Museum of Modern Art, New York. His travels continued in 1945 with visits and exhibitions in the capital cities of Peru, Chile, Argentina, and Bolivia. Murals executed by Guayasamin depict historical and universal themes such as *The History of Man and His Culture, Discovery of the Amazon River,* and *Homage to the American Man.* Since the 1960s his art has been included in more than 150 group shows and one-man exhibitions throughout the world. He is represented in many private and public collections in the United States and South America.

7. Ida Kohlmeyer (b. 1912)

Ida Kohlmeyer was born in New Orleans, Louisiana on November 3, 1912. A graduate of Newcomb College, New Orleans, she continued her studies in 1956 with Hans Hofmann. From 1956 to 1964 she was on the faculty of Newcomb College, and in 1973 and 1974 was a visiting professor of art at Louisiana State University, New Orleans. The artist's abstract and symbolic compositions have been exhibited throughout the United States in one-woman exhibitions at the New Orleans Museum of Art (formerly the Delgado Museum), New Orleans; Sheldon Memorial Art Gallery, Nebraska; the High Museum of Art, Georgia; and others. Group exhibitions in which she has participated include the 1963 and 1967 Biennial of Contemporary American Painting at the Corcoran Gallery of Art, Washington, D.C.; *Art Across America,* Knoedler Galleries, New York; Third Bienal de Arte Coltejar, Medellin, Columbia, South America; and *American Women - 20th Century,* Lakeview Center for the Arts and Sciences, Illinois. She has been awarded prizes at the Artist's Annual, New Orleans Museum of Art; Chautauqua National Exhibition of American Painting, New York; the 28th Corcoran Biennial of American Painting; and the High Museum. Paintings by Ida Kohlmeyer are in many public and private collections. She currently makes her home in New Orleans.

8. Virginia R. Rogers (20th cen.)

Virginia R. Rogers was born in Coronado, California. The painter studied in New York with Guiseppi Trotta; with Jim Tidmore in San Antonio, Texas; and with John Wagnon and Barbara Gallagher in Montgomery, Alabama. Her realistic flower paintings and still lifes have been exhibited in local exhibitions and awarded several prizes. Mrs. Rogers presently resides in Ohio.

9. John Wagnon (b. 1933)

John Wagnon was born in Montgomery, Alabama on February 9, 1933. He was awarded a Bachelor of Arts Degree in History from the University of Alabama and is widely known throughout the region. The artist has taken classes with the Montgomery Art Guild, and has achieved a significant reputation from painting the Alabama landscape and scenes inspired from his home town of Montgomery. In October of 1973 he was given a one-man exhibition at the Montgomery Museum of Fine Arts. His work is in numerous Montgomery private collections and is also included in the Union Bank collection and the Montgomery Museum of Fine Arts Association collection. The artist presently resides in Montgomery where he serves on the Board of the Montgomery Museum of Fine Arts Association, and is president of the Montgomery Art Guild.

10. Clark Walker (b. 1940)

Clark Walker was born in Selma, Alabama on June 7, 1940. In 1960 the artist began his art studies with Charles Shannon of the University of Alabama. During the summer of 1962 he studied at The Art Students League of New York; the summers of 1963 and 1966 were spent at the Skowhegan School of Painting, Maine where he studied with Ben Shahn and Jack Levine and was awarded the Bocour Award. From 1963 to 1965 he served in the United States Army in Germany. Since his return he has maintained a studio in Montgomery. The artist has received numerous awards in Southern local and regional exhibitions such as the Southeastern Exhibition in Atlanta, the Alabama State Fair, and the Alabama Art League. He exhibited in the joint Faculty-Alumni show of the Skowhegan School of Painting held in New York City in 1967.

Weil Brothers-Cotton, Inc.

Thomas Hart Benton, N.A.   *Across the Curve of the Road*

Charles Burchfield

Blossoming Trees

Carroll Cloar

Lull in the Revolution

Winslow Homer, N.A.   *Upland Cotton*

Maurice Utrillo

La Caserne

Andrew Wyeth, N.A.   *Alexander Chandler*

CATALOG*

1. Thomas Hart Benton, N.A. (1889-1975)
   Across the Curve of the Road
   23¹/₂ x 29¹/₂
   Oil on canvas

2. Charles Burchfield (1893-1967)
   Blossoming Trees
   19 x 25¹/₂
   Watercolor

3. Carroll Cloar (b. 1913)
   Lull in the Revolution
   17³/₄ x 23¹/₂
   Tempera on masonite

4. Eugene Conlon (b. 1925)
   Meeting House
   21¹/₂ x 29¹/₂
   Watercolor

5. Winslow Homer, N.A. (1836-1910)
   Upland Cotton
   49 x 29¹/₄
   Oil on canvas

6. Willem de Kooning (b. 1904)
   Woman
   26¹/₄ x 10¹/₂
   Oil on paper

7. Berthe Morisot (1841-1895)
   La Seine en Aval au Pont d'Lena
   19¹/₂ x 31
   Oil on canvas

8. Maurice Utrillo (1883-1955)
   La Caserne
   20³/₄ x 25¹/₄
   Oil on canvas

9. Andrew Wyeth, N.A. (b. 1917)
   Alexander Chandler
   20³/₄ x 14
   Watercolor

10. Andrew Wyeth, N.A. (b. 1917)
    Charley Irving
    14 x 20
    Watercolor

* Dimensions are given in inches.
Height precedes width.

BIOGRAPHIES

1. Thomas Hart Benton, N.A. (1889-1975)

Thomas Hart Benton was born in Neosho, Missouri on April 15, 1889. His art studies began at The Art Institute of Chicago and were continued at the Académie Julian in Paris. At this time his friendship with Stanton McDonald-Wright resulted in his involvement with the avant-garde Synchromist movement and participation in the *Forum Exhibition of Modern American Painters* of 1916. He returned to the United States in 1912 and from 1926 to 1955 taught at The Art Students League of New York where he had Jackson Pollock and Fairfield Porter as pupils. In the late 1920s he executed his first mural commissions utilizing the techniques of the Mexican fresco painters but characterized by typical American subjects. Murals were painted by the artist for the New School of Social Research, New York; the Hall of States, Chicago Century of Progress Exposition; the Missouri State Capitol; and others. Extensive travels in the South and Midwest provided visual material for paintings of the 1930s when Benton became a leading exponent of the Regionalist school of painting. He was Director of Painting, Kansas City Art Institute and School of Design, Missouri for six years and was an artist-reporter for *Life, St. Louis Post Dispatch,* and *Kansas City (Missouri) Star.* His views on art were expressed in two books he authored, *Artist in America* and *An American in Art.* Retrospectives of the artist's work have been held at the Joslyn Art Museum, Nebraska; The New Britain Museum of American Art, Connecticut; Indiana University Museum, Bloomington; and others. Benton was a member of the National Institute of Arts and Letters and the American Academy of Arts and Letters. His work has been included in numerous group shows and is represented in public and private collections in the United States and Europe. The artist died in 1975.

2. Charles Burchfield (1893-1967)

See Blount, Inc. No. 1.

3. Carroll Cloar (b. 1913)

Carroll Cloar was born in Earle, Arkansas on January 18, 1913. He received his Bachelor of Arts degree from Southwestern College, Memphis in 1934. This was followed by additional study at the Memphis Academy of Arts and The Art Students League of New York with William C. McNulty and Harry Sternberg. In 1940 he received the MacDowell Colony Fellowship, and he was awarded a Guggenheim Foundation Fellowship in 1946. After completion of his military service during World War II, he traveled for four years throughout Central and South America. The subjects of his paintings derive from this experience as well as from his earlier background in Arkansas and Tennessee. He has exhibited extensively in both group and one-man shows at the Whitney Museum of American Art, New York; the Brooks Memorial Art Gallery, Memphis; the Fort Worth Art Museum, Texas; and others. Retrospectives have been mounted at the Brooks Memorial Art Gallery, State University of New York at Albany, and Kennedy Galleries, New York. In 1966 he was awarded a grant from the National Institute of Arts and Letters and the American Academy of Arts and Letters. Works by the artist are in numerous collections including The Brooklyn Museum; the Corcoran Gallery of Art, Washington, D.C.; the Hirshhorn Museum and Sculpture Garden, Washington, D.C.; The Museum of Modern Art, New York; and the Library of Congress. Carroll Cloar presently resides in Memphis, Tennessee.

4. Eugene Conlon (b. 1925)

Eugene Conlon was born in Boston, Massachusetts in 1925. He graduated from the Massachusetts College of Art in 1950 with a Bachelor of Fine Arts degree. He has been employed as a designer, illustrator, watercolor instructor, and technical artist. His watercolors have been exhibited in museums and galleries throughout the United States such as the Boston Museum of Fine Arts; Museum of Fine Arts, Missouri; The Allied Artists Show, New York; and the Quandrangle Galleries, Dallas.

Shows in which the artist has been given prizes and honorable mentions include the South Shore Art Festival, Massachusetts and the Boston Art Directors Club. He is a member of the Boston Water Color Society, the South Shores Art Association, and the Cambridge Art Association.

5. Winslow Homer, N.A. (1836-1910)

Winslow Homer was born in Boston, Massachusetts on February 24, 1836. At the age of nineteen he was apprenticed to lithographer John H. Bufford of Boston where he executed designs for sheet music and greeting cards. Two years later he began his twenty-year career as a free-lance illustrator for periodicals such as *Ballou's Pictorial* and *Harper's Weekly.* His formal art studies were at a Brooklyn drawing school and briefly at the National Academy of Design. He covered the Virginia Front of the Civil War as a correspondent-artist for *Harper's Weekly* prior to an extended visit to Paris. Homer was elected an academician of the National Academy of Design in 1865 and frequently exhibited in the annual exhibitions. The seacoast town of Tynemouth in England was his home for the years 1881 and 1882 and it was from this time that most of his marine pictures date. Upon his return to the United States, he settled in Prout's Neck, Maine where he remained until his death in 1910 except for travels to Nassau and Bermuda. During his lifetime he participated in shows in Paris, England, and the United States and one-man shows of his work were hung in Boston and New York. He was a member of the American Society of Painters of Watercolors and in 1893 received the Gold Medal, World's Columbian Exposition, Chicago. Posthumous exhibitions include a memorial exhibition at The Metropolitan Museum of Art, New York; a centenary exhibition at the Whitney Museum of American Art, New York; and a retrospective at the National Gallery of Art, Washington, D.C.

He is represented in the aforementioned museum collections; the Museum of Fine Arts, Boston; The Art Institute of Chicago; and others.

6. Willem de Kooning (b. 1904)

Willem de Kooning was born in Rotterdam, The Netherlands on April 24, 1904. During his youth he was apprenticed to a commercial art firm and studied at the Rotterdam Academy of Fine Arts in the evenings. In 1926 he came to the United States where he worked as a house painter, free-lance commercial artist, stage designer, and decorator until 1935 when he found employment with the WPA Federal Art Project Easel and Mural Divisions, New York. Although he showed in several group exhibitions in the 1930s and 1940s, his first one-man show was not held until 1948. He has taught at Black Mountain College, North Carolina and Yale University. In 1951 he began the *Women* series in which the female image was abstracted and used as a medium to explore spatial and color relationships and tensions. As one of America's foremost Abstract Expressionists, he has exhibited in the Venice Biennale; *Abstract Painting and Sculpture in America,* The Museum of Modern Art, New York; I and II São Paolo Bienal; *The New Decade,* Whitney Museum of American Art, New York; and *Painting and Sculpture of a Decade, 54-64,* The Tate Gallery, London. Retrospectives of de Kooning's art have been hung at the School of the Museum of Fine Arts, Boston; the Massachusetts Institute of Technology; and The Museum of Modern Art, International Circulating Exhibition. Among the awards he has received are the Logan Medal, The Art Institute of Chicago; Freedom Award Medal, presented by President Lyndon B. Johnson; and the Brandeis University Creative Arts Award Medal. The artist presently resides in New York.

7. Berthe Morisot (1841-1895)

Berthe Morisot was born in Bourges, France on January 14, 1841. Her first drawing lessons were under the instruction of Monsieur Chocarne; J. B. Guichard was her second teacher. In 1861 she met Corot who influenced and encouraged her early works. She was introduced to Edouard Manet by Fantin-Latour in 1868 and later married Manet's younger brother Eugène. Morisot and Edouard Manet had a mutual influence on each other's painting style. Both artists always retained some technical aspects that were non-impressionistic, in particular, a concern with composition over color optical experimentation. In 1864 Morisot exhibited in the Salon for the first time. She also participated in the first Impressionist Exhibition in 1874 and each subsequent Impressionist Exhibition except for the one held in 1879. Her oils and pastels of landscapes and domestic scenes are included in the collections of major museums in Europe and the United States. The artist died in Paris in 1895.

8. Maurice Utrillo (1893-1955)

Maurice Utrillo was born in Paris on December 25, 1883. The illegitimate son of Suzanne Valadon, a painter and model for the French painters Renoir, Degas, and Toulouse-Lautrec, the boy was adopted by the Spanish artist Miguel Utrillo who gave him his first art lessons. Utrillo began drinking at an early age and was to be troubled by alcoholism for many years. He was first encouraged to paint by his mother as a form of therapy. His most successful art, often scenes of Montmartre and other city and architectural views, was painted during his *White Period,* 1908-1914. Despite his personal tormented existence during these years, his paintings expressed a calm and delicate feeling. He participated in the Salon d'Automne of 1909 and his first one-man exhibition was hung in 1913. In 1928 he was made a Chevalier of The Legion of Honour; in 1935 he married Mme. Pauwels. In his later years he controlled his drinking and lived a normal life, but his work became repetitious and the quality decreased. Most major museums of modern art have examples of his work. The artist died at Le Vésinet on November 5, 1955.

9. Andrew Wyeth, N.A. (b. 1917)

Andrew Wyeth was born at Chadds Ford, Pennsylvania on July 21, 1917. He began studying art at an early age under the tutelage of his father N. C. Wyeth, a painter and illustrator, and at the age of twelve Andrew did illustrations for the Brandywine Edition of *Robin Hood.* Wyeth's realistic paintings, which often express a psychological and physical loneliness, have been hung in many one-man shows. The first was held at the Macbeth Gallery in New York in 1937 and other shows have since been hung in Boston, San Francisco, Washington, D.C., and New York. He has received honorary doctorates from Harvard University, Colby College, Dickinson College, and Swarthmore College as well as awards from the American Academy of Arts and Letters and the National Institute of Arts and Letters. The National Academy of Design elected him an academician in 1944. He is a member of the Audubon Artists, the National Institute of Arts and Letters, and the American Academy of Arts and Letters. His work is represented in numerous public and private collections including the California Palace of the Legion of Honor; the Dallas Museum of Fine Arts; the Wadsworth Atheneum, Connecticut; The Museum of Modern Art, New York; and the Philadelphia Museum of Art. The artist lives in Chadds Ford in the winter and summers in Cushing, Maine.

10. Andrew Wyeth
See No. 9.

INDEX OF ARTISTS

Italicized page numbers indicate illustration.

This catalog was designed by Lou and Julie Toffaletti, Montgomery, Alabama.

Six hundred copies were produced by Pioneer Press, Inc., Montgomery, Alabama for the Montgomery Museum of Fine Arts in April of 1976.

Photographs are by Loren Mears, Orlando, Florida. Halftones are by Color Craft, Inc., Montgomery, Alabama.

The type face used is Helvetica, set by Compos-it, Inc., Montgomery, Alabama.

Cover stock is Weyerhaeuser Carousel white 80 lb. cover. The divider pages are Carousel white 80 lb. text. The inside stock is Warren Patina, 80 lb. text.